The Small Business

Strategic Planning Workbook

for 2020

Also by Dave Ferguson

The Business Owners Bible, Operating on Faith

KEEP THE FAITH!

The Small Business Strategic Planning Workbook for 2020

Dave Ferguson

LCBC

Lake County Business Coaching, Inc., Publisher

Libertyville, Illinois

Disclaimer: While the strategies described in this book have proved successful, not every one of them is appropriate for all individuals, businesses or situations. Strategic decisions are the responsibility of the reader.

ISBN: 9781701558175

This book is dedicated to all the business owners who have taken the time to do the planning required to build the business of their dreams. Without their efforts, no one would believe that having a plan could make a difference. People who believe make the effort to achieve.

Table of Contents

INTRODUCTION TO THE 2020 EDITION

I know you have goals. If you didn't, you wouldn't be reading this. You want to do something to achieve those goals. You want help and that's why I created this workbook and why I've updated the content and added the What If's chapter for the 2020 edition.

In my workshops, when I introduce a group of business owners to Strategic Planning, I'll set the scene by saying:

> *"I assume you all have goals for your business, right?"* (Everyone nods.) *"Now, are they really goals or just dreams? Remember, dreams are goals without deadlines. Maybe they're more like fantasies - dreams without a deadline or a plan. I hope none of you are living a nightmare. That's working without a plan, or goals, or a schedule."*

Whatever your situation, this workbook is intended to help. It evolved from the full day Strategic Planning Workshop I developed for small business owners. After doing the workshop several times, seeing the way it changed the thinking – and the results – of the participants, I knew it needed to be in a format that any small business owner could use anywhere and anytime to improve their results.

Most of the small business owners I work with don't have the time to spend a full day away from their business. This workbook will give you the flexibility to work on each section as you have time. One word of warning though: Plan to spend at least an hour of uninterrupted time when you work on a section. It's intended to help your thinking - not your doing - and good thinking takes time.

Finally, this is not a substitute for a business plan. This is the work you do before you write a business plan and the work you do before you revise it each year. It doesn't have to be perfect, you won't be graded on appearance or spelling. No one will see it unless you want to show it to them, so have fun. It will be a journey of discovery – and commitment. You'll need a few tools to make your journey more effective: a yellow highlighter, a blue highlighter, pencils and pens (including red), a calculator, and a pad of small sticky notes. This is a workbook and, if you do the work, it will reflect it. Cross things out, erase one comment to replace it with a better one. Add thoughts and calculations and save your sticky notes on the NOTES pages at the end of the workbook. It might be confusing and frustrating. It might be a bit messy. Don't give up, the results will justify the effort.

The following illustration shows the process we will be following in the workbook. We'll start with where you are now and look ahead to where you want to be in the future – we'll be moving from Here to There.

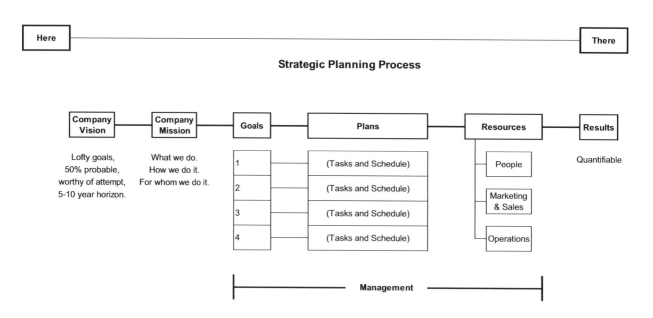

The first chapter will explain the process in more detail.

WHAT IS A STRATEGIC PLAN?

For business owners, planning should be strategic. Like a military general, your mission is to win the war. You look at the field of battle and develop plans to achieve your targets. You might not win every battle, but by achieving most of your targets you will reach your goal.

In business, the field of battle is constantly changing. Your targets are moving and so is your competition. You can't continue doing what you've always done - unless you are willing to get what you've always gotten. Strategic planning in business is looking at the whole competitive landscape, recognizing what is happening now and making some assumptions about what will probably happen in the future. Based on that planning you can position your resources where they will be most effective and take action at the right time.

Strategic planning isn't difficult. When I work with people I use a five-step process. The illustration in the introduction shows how we move through the process, getting from where we are to where we want to be.

We begin with an understanding of the company's vision. What do you want the company to look like in a year, or five years? Though you might not realize your ultimate vision, you can't achieve lofty goals by aiming low. Aim for what you want.

The next step in the process is to develop your mission - describe what you do, how you do it and for whom. You should have lofty goals, but we'll narrow our focus to be more effective and create a high probability of success. You can't do, or be, everything for everyone.

The third step is to set specific goals for the year. While gross revenue is important, net profit is even more important. Yet, revenue and profit are dependent on customers and transactions. How many customers will you need and what average transaction amount will allow you to achieve your goals? How many prospects will you need to work with to convert them to customers? How will you find those prospects?

The next step is one that is frequently ignored. We need to look at how the goals will affect the company in terms of resources over the coming year. If you want to increase sales by 20 percent, do you have the people and capacity to handle that increased load? How will your marketing approach and budget need to change to generate those new sales? Will new training or equipment be required? How will all the changes affect cash flow? What will need to be done and when?

The last step in the process is to re-balance the goals and the resources. The approach here is to optimize the use of resources and make sure the goals are achievable. Business owners often want to maximize every resource, but their resources are interdependent. Employees can't act until people make decisions or provide information, funding is limited, and your customers will make decisions when it suits them, not you. While we can't maximize effectively, we can optimize. To optimize means choosing the most advantageous approach. Balancing the goals and the resources with the schedule will achieve the best results given the limitations of those resources.

The strategic plan, when completed, becomes a framework for creating the more detailed planning and projects that become the daily activities that support the goals. Conflicts are minimized, and costs are controlled. Results become more predictable. Isn't that an investment worth making?

BACKGROUND INFORMATION

We will first need to understand where we are if we want to decide where we're going. This section is devoted to describing the present. It's required to create effective mission and vision statements. More importantly, unless you understand where you are, you won't know how to get where you're going. Over the next few pages we are going to develop the Vision and Mission Statements. These are intended to communicate in very few words where you are headed and why. We'll start by exploring some underlying factors that will allow you to see the bigger picture and then describe it clearly.

We'll start with personal factors and then move on to business factors. Take your time. The better you can describe these, the more powerful - and more accurate - your vision and mission statements will be.

About You

Why did you start this business?

- _____
- _____
- _____
- _____

What do you like about the business?

- _____
- _____
- _____
- _____

What do you dislike about the business?

- _____
- _____
- _____
- _____

What do you like about your role?

- _____
- _____
- _____
- _____

What do you dislike about your role?

- _____
- _____
- _____
- _____

What are your personal values? (Consult the list at the end of this section.)

- _____
- _____
- _____
- _____

What limiting beliefs keep you from taking action? (I'm not smart enough, I don't have the expertise, I'm not a leader, I can't sell, etc.) List each limiting belief.

- _____
- _____
- _____
- _____
- _____
- _____

Since these are merely beliefs, circle those that could be eliminated with education or training.

What behaviors keep you from doing what you need to? (Lack of planning, too many distractions, lack of priorities, difficulty managing time, etc.)

- _____
- _____
- _____
- _____

What personal FUDS (Fears, Uncertainties, Doubts and Suppositions) keep you from taking action?

- _____
- _____
- _____
- _____

What is your exit strategy? How do you plan to exit the business and when? (Sell it, turn it over to family members, close it, I don't have one, etc.)

- _____
- _____
- _____
- _____
- _____
- _____
- _____

Values List Exercise 1

In the list below circle your personal values.

Adaptable	Diligent	Joyful	Respectful
Appreciative	Discernment	Kind	Responsible
Attentive	Discrete	Leadership	Safety
Available	Efficient	Loving	Security
Careful	Equitable	Loyal	Self-Control
Commitment	Fair	Meek	Sincere
Committed	Faithful	Merciful	Submissive
Compassion	Fearless	Observant	Tactful
Concern	Flexible	Optimistic	Teamwork
Confidence	Forgiving	Patient	Temperance
Consideration	Friendly	Peaceful	Thorough
Consistency	Frugal	Perseverance	Thrifty
Contentment	Generous	Persistence	Tolerant
Cooperative	Gentle	Persuasive	Trustworthy
Creative	Grateful	Prudent	Truthful
Decisive	Honest	Punctual	Uncomplaining
Deferent	Humble	Purpose	Understanding
Dependable	Humility	Reliable	Virtuous
Determined	Integrity	Resourceful	

Remember that your values are reflective of your personality. While your personality is difficult to change, your behavior isn't. While you can't change your feelings, you can change your behavior - your response to those feelings - at any time to suit the occasion. You might want to search online for the Riso-Hudson Enneagram Type Indicator test to see what your personality type is. It might influence how you see your business and work with people. The online test is free. I'm a Type 1, no surprise there.

About Your Business

What is your product or service?

- _____
- _____
- _____
- _____

What solutions do you provide? What problems do you solve? How do you actually help your customers?

- _____
- _____
- _____
- _____
- _____

Who are your customers?

- _____
- _____
- _____
- _____

Why do they (or would they) do business with you?

- _____
- _____
- _____
- _____

Why do customers choose not to do business with you? (They might choose to do business with your competition, spend their money on something else, or not spend it at all)

- _____
- _____
- _____
- _____

How do your customers communicate with you?

- _____
- _____
- _____
- _____

How do you communicate with your customers?

- _____
- _____
- _____
- _____

What are your revenue streams? (What are the major product or service categories that you should track individually?)

- _____
- _____
- _____
- _____

What are the strengths of your business?
(Financial, staff, resources, communication, management)

- _____
- _____
- _____
- _____

What are the weaknesses of your business? (Financial, staff, resources, communication, management)

- _____
- _____
- _____
- _____

What opportunities do you see for your business?
(Market, products, services, technology, demographics)

- _____
- _____
- _____
- _____

What threats currently exist?
(Competition, technology, governmental, legal, etc.)

- _____
- _____
- _____
- _____

What threats might arise in the future and when?

- _____
- _____
- _____
- _____

How does your business benefit the planet and its inhabitants?

- _____
- _____
- _____
- _____

Are there any other important factors that should be considered? List them here.

- _____
- _____
- _____
- _____

In the organization chart that follows, fill in the names of the people responsible for the departments shown. Feel free to re-draw the chart to suit your business organization remembering that all the major functions shown are typically required of any business. If you outsource responsibilities like accounting, fill in the name of the organization or individual you that will be responsible for that department.

Having your name in more than one box is an indication that you have too many day to day responsibilities to effectively manage your business.

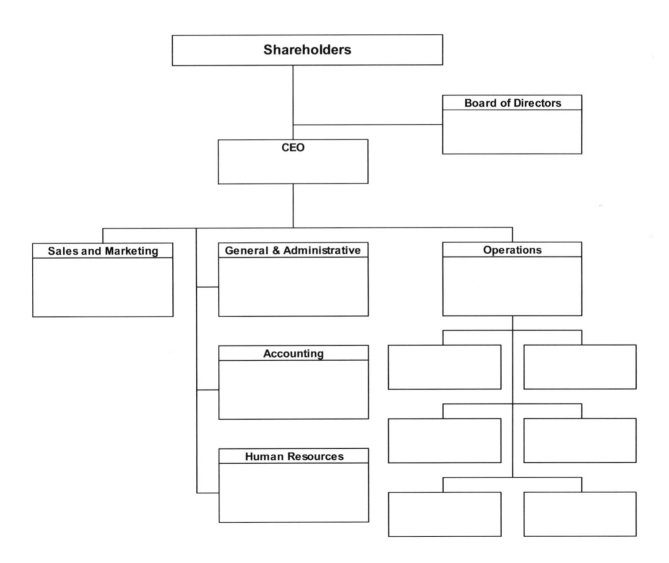

VISION

As we see from the chart in the Introduction, Vision is about the future. It's a big picture view of where the company is headed. It's what you imagine in your dreams, not what you confront every day. It's also the picture your employees, vendors, and customers need to clearly understand. As a business owner, you need everyone onboard and heading in the same direction if you want to reach your goals.

Because it's a big picture view and because it envisions things that might not even exist right now, it's important to find a way to "work" on your vision without interruption. The first questions are intended to stimulate your imagination. Then we'll move into some questions to focus your thinking. By doing the exercises you'll find it much easier to craft a Vision Statement that makes sense for you and for your business.

Please allow yourself the freedom to imagine even the seemingly impossible. This is not the time to worry about the market, customers, expenses, or profitability. We'll spend plenty of time and effort on that later in the process. This is the time to think outside the box, to indulge your passion, and to dream.

One of the exercises I do in my workshops is to ask everyone to relax, close their eyes, and imagine their business 5 years from now. Imagine yourself in a room where the activity of your business is taking place. What does it look like? What does it sound like? What does it smell like? What are people doing and saying? How does it feel? What brings energy to the space? Spend 5 minutes creating this film clip in your imagination. Does it feel possible? Of course it does, you just imagined it. Now all we need to do is put that into a few words.

In the next section focus on your future vision of your business and answer the questions. This is not the time to worry about how we will get there. Rather, it's about where we want to be.

What are your revenue streams and how much revenue will each contribute in the coming year?

- _____
- _____
- _____
- _____
- _____
- _____

What will your total revenue be from all streams?

- _____

How many new customers will you need to generate this revenue?

- _____
- _____
- _____
- _____

How many employees will you need to generate this revenue?

- _____
- _____
- _____
- _____

Why would new employees want to join your organization?

- _____
- _____
- _____
- _____

Why would current employees want to stay with your organization?

- _____
- _____
- _____
- _____

What characteristics will attract customers to you?

- _____
- _____
- _____
- _____

How will you attract customers away from your competition?

- _____
- _____
- _____
- _____

How will your work positively impact the world?

- _____
- _____
- _____

How will your work contribute to the aspirations of your employees and vendors?

- _____
- _____
- _____

What three words would you use to describe the company you envision?

- _____
- _____
- _____

What three words would your customers use to describe the company you envision?

- _____
- _____
- _____

Why will your customers want to do business with you?

- _____
- _____
- _____

Why will your employees want to work for you?

- _____
- _____
- _____

In three sentences describe your vision.

_____

_____

_____

_____

_____

_____

_____

_____

_____

_____

Now, cross out all the meaningless modifiers and marketing jargon in the three sentences above and write your vision in one sentence that everyone can understand, remember, and repeat.

_____

_____

_____

_____

_____

_____

_____

_____

_____

_____

MISSION

Mission is what you will do now to achieve your long-term vision. This is what you intend to accomplish going forward, so it is stated in such a way that people recognize when they have accomplished what they set out to do. The mission needs to be clear, and simple enough that every employee can recognize how their decisions fit within the bigger picture.

To have an effective mission you need to understand your own capabilities, who your customers are, and what differentiates you from your competition.

What do we do?

- _____
- _____
- _____
- _____

How do we do it?

- _____
- _____
- _____
- _____

For whom do we do it?

- _____
- _____
- _____
- _____

How do we differentiate ourselves?

- _____
- _____
- _____
- _____

How do we retain customers?

- _____
- _____
- _____
- _____

How do we measure success?

- _____
- _____
- _____
- _____

From the answers above, circle the five most important factors.

Write three short sentences that embrace those ideas.

_____
_____
_____
_____
_____
_____
_____
_____
_____
_____

Now, cross out all the meaningless modifiers and marketing jargon in the three sentences above and write your mission in one sentence that everyone can understand, remember, and repeat.

_____

_____

_____

_____

_____

_____

_____

_____

_____

_____

VALUES

Values are about how you do business, how you treat your customers and your employees, how your employees treat each other, and how you are perceived by the public. Values are a constant, they don't change with the economy or the weather. Values are something to be embraced, taught, lived by and passed on.

The worksheet on the following page will help you to define these.

Values List Exercise 2

Highlight your company's values with a blue highlighter. Highlight your customers' values with a yellow highlighter. Those that show as green are shared values - your company values align with customer values. Now, underline the values you embrace in your organization.

Adaptable	Diligent	Joyful	Respectful
Appreciative	Discernment	Kind	Responsible
Attentive	Discrete	Leadership	Safety
Available	Efficient	Loving	Security
Careful	Equitable	Loyal	Self-Control
Commitment	Fair	Meek	Sincere
Committed	Faithful	Merciful	Submissive
Compassion	Fearless	Observant	Tactful
Concern	Flexible	Optimistic	Teamwork
Confidence	Forgiving	Patient	Temperance
Consideration	Friendly	Peaceful	Thorough
Consistency	Frugal	Perseverance	Thrifty
Contentment	Generous	Persistence	Tolerant
Cooperative	Gentle	Persuasive	Trustworthy
Creative	Grateful	Prudent	Truthful
Decisive	Honest	Punctual	Uncomplaining
Deferent	Humble	Purpose	Understanding
Dependable	Humility	Resourceful	Virtuous
Determined	Integrity		

Go back and review your personal values from the Values List Exercise 1 in Chapter 2, then answer the following questions.

From the Values List, what are the company's values?

- _____
- _____
- _____
- _____

From the Values List, what are the customers' values?

- _____
- _____
- _____
- _____

What values are held in common by you, your customers and your organization?

- _____
- _____
- _____
- _____

What values are not held in common? For each, decide if it is, or is not, important. Circle your decision.

- _____ Is/ Is Not
- _____ Is/ Is Not
- _____ Is/ Is Not
- _____ Is/ Is Not
- _____ Is/ Is Not

Write three to five phrases that summarize your company's values. We believe in:

- _____
- _____
- _____
- _____
- _____

GOALS

At this point you've done enough thinking to establish goals for the business. Goals take many forms: profit, growth, revenue, market share, giving back to the community, etc. Your goals should reflect your vision of the company's possibilities.

Start with revenue. Think about the business from the standpoint of revenue streams - distinct sources of revenue that can actually be managed. Total revenue would be all those individual streams added together.

Profit is a simple calculation, revenue less expenses. Gross profit is revenue less the cost of goods sold, a simple measure of performance. A better measure of performance is Net Income - what remains after all expenses are paid. That's what determines how much income you receive.

Expenses are the costs of running the business and are often referred to as overhead. They include rent, utilities, insurance, office supplies, labor, interest, transportation, and marketing to name a few. Some are discretionary, all should be monitored.

Remember that, all things being equal, your net income each year should increase to account for the effects of inflation. Inflation is running at about 2% as of this writing. Raising prices is an alternative, or lowering costs, but workers expect their wages to increase to account for the effect of inflation. The things they need cost more. The same is true for you.

You might also have important personal goals that will become part of the plan. Controlling the number of hours you spend working IN the business instead of ON the business will affect the number of hours others will need to spend on management tasks. That's where the notion of FTE's, Full Time

Equivalent's comes into play. It doesn't matter if people are working full time or part time, simply divide total labor hours by 40 to get that number.

Once you've determined your goals for the next year, incorporate those goals in the cash flow forecast that follows.

Strategic Goals for Next Year

_____Revenue _____

_____Revenue _____

_____Revenue _____

_____Revenue _____

Total Revenue _____

Gross Profit _____

Net Income _____

Work hours/Week _____

FTE employees   _____

Objectives

These might be things that can't be measured easily such as increasing efficiency, smoothing the revenue stream to eliminate peaks and valleys during the year, or taking more vacation time.

- _____
- _____
- _____
- _____

Strategic Goals for Year Two

_____Revenue _____

_____Revenue _____

_____Revenue _____

_____Revenue _____

Total Revenue _____

Gross Profit _____

Net Income _____

Work hours/Week _____

FTE employees   _____

Objectives

- _____
- _____
- _____
- _____

Strategic Goals for Year Three

_____Revenue _____
_____Revenue _____
_____Revenue _____
_____Revenue _____
Total Revenue _____
Gross Profit _____
Net Income _____
Work hours/Week _____
FTE employees   _____

Objectives

- _____
- _____
- _____
- _____

Strategic Goals for Year Four

_____Revenue _____

_____Revenue _____

_____Revenue _____

_____Revenue _____

Total Revenue _____

Gross Profit _____

Net Income _____

Work hours/Week _____

FTE employees   _____

Objectives

- _____

- _____

- _____

- _____

Strategic Goals for Year Five

_____Revenue _____
_____Revenue _____
_____Revenue _____
_____Revenue _____
Total Revenue _____
Gross Profit _____
Net Income _____
Work hours/Week _____
FTE employees   _____

Objectives

- _____
- _____
- _____
- _____

PROJECTED CASH FLOW

	January	February	March	April	May	June
CASH						
Beginning Cash						
Revenue stream 1						
Revenue stream 2						
Revenue stream 3						
TOTAL CASH RECEIVED						
EXPENSES						
Purchase of Inventory						
COGS (Cost Of Goods Sold)						
Salaries and Wages						
Burden (FICA, Vacation, Ins)						
Other Employee Expenses						
Utilities						
Rent/Lease						
Office Supplies						
Telephones						
Printing/Photocopying						
Misc. (including postage)						
Marketing/Advertising						
Insurance						
Auto/Transportation						
Travel/Entertainment						
Local Taxes/Licenses						
Packaging/Shipping						
Subscriptions/Dues						
Bank Charges						
Interest						
Commissions						
Decorating						
Legal/Accounting						
Other - List						
TOTAL EXPENSES						
CASH AVAILABLE						
Owner compensation						
Payment on Debt						
ENDING CASH						

July	August	September	October	November	December	Annual Total	
							CASH
							Beginning Cash
							Revenue stream 1
							Revenue stream 2
							Revenue stream 3
							TOTAL CASH RECEIVED
							EXPENSES
							Purchase of Inventory
							COGS (Cost Of Goods Sold)
							Salaries and Wages
							Burden (FICA, Vacation, Ins)
							Other Employee Expenses
							Utilities
							Rent/Lease
							Office Supplies
							Telephones
							Printing/Photocopying
							Misc. (including postage)
							Marketing/Advertising
							Insurance
							Auto/Transportation
							Travel/Entertainment
							Local Taxes/Licenses
							Packaging/Shipping
							Subscriptions/Dues
							Bank Charges
							Interest
							Commissions
							Decorating
							Legal/Accounting
							Other - List
							TOTAL EXPENSES
							CASH AVAILABLE
							Owner compensation
							Payment on Debt
							ENDING CASH

MARKETING

Marketing is the process of educating your customers. It boils down to getting their attention and interest. Sales is getting their money, so without the marketing component there won't be any sales.

What tools are you using now? Are they communicating to your target market? Based on your responses to the questions you've answered so far, are there target markets that should be added to your list of marketing initiatives?

On the following pages list the target markets and strategies you have in mind. Note the strategies that are working well now but also consider new strategies, especially those that might be effective for your competition. Your strategies might include:
- Customer touches by mail, email, phone, or in person
- Networking at referral groups, chamber events, industry associations, or casual events
- Social Media
- Advertising in print, online or through broadcast media
- Trade shows
- Seasonal promotions
- Customer appreciation events
- Consumer education events
- Special events or celebrations

Don't worry about the details at this point, the objective is to get as many ideas as possible down on paper. Evaluating those ideas will be the next step in the process.

Target Market _____
Strategy:

- _____
- _____
- _____
- _____
- _____

Target Market _____
Strategy:

- _____
- _____
- _____
- _____
- _____

Target Market _____
Strategy:

- _____
- _____
- _____
- _____
- _____

Target Market _____
Strategy:

- _____
- _____
- _____
- _____
- _____

Target Market _____
Strategy:

- _____
- _____
- _____
- _____
- _____

Target Market _____
Strategy:

- _____
- _____
- _____
- _____
- _____

Not every marketing initiative will have a positive return on investment. Some will be intended to differentiate, build awareness, or announce company changes. Those are an investment in the company's reputation. For those that are intended to generate sales, it's important to track the return on your investment of time and money. To decide which marketing projects will make financial sense, do a preliminary analysis using the spreadsheet which follows. Based on the return you calculate - and the time and effort required from you and your staff - implement those ideas that will generate the highest return. In the following spreadsheet, Gross Profit is the Converted responses times the Profit on each response and ROI is calculated as (Gross Profit minus Total Cost) divided by Total Cost.

Initiative	Date	Target Market	Quantity Out	Unit Cost	Total Cost	Responses	Converted	Profit Each	Gross Profit	ROI
Direct mail offer	2/5	Households < 3 miles	20000 Post cards	0.35	7000	400	100	100	10000	43%
Magazine Ad	3/7	Metro area affluent	10000 circulation	0.12	1200 Ad cost	50	20	100	2000	67%

No matter the initiative you have in mind, each can be evaluated based on your return on investment using industry-standard response rates and your own conversion statistics.

The marketing initiatives you pursue will require time and effort, so use the calendar form on the following pages to lay out a complete schedule that makes sense for your business. The calendar has been laid out so that the day of the week aligns vertically to make recurring weekly events easier to enter.

Using highlighters and colored pencils will help you to visualize the schedule and balance activities during the year to minimize stress on the organization. Show holidays and any other events that affect availability. Block out the days when the business will not be open. Put in your planned vacation time.

Businesses with seasonal activities require adequate lead time for marketing activities designed to generate sales during the season. The same holds true for businesses that have specific cash flow requirements.

Put in reporting, tax, and any other deadlines that you are required – or want – to meet. The goal of this exercise is to think through the year now so that critical activities can be completed in a timely, stress-free and pro-active way.

2020

Day of Week	Wed	Thur	Fri	Sat	Sun	Mon	Tue	Wed	Thur	Fri	Sat	Sun	Mon	Tue	Wed	Thur	Fri
January	1	2	3	4	5	6	7	8	9	10	11	12	13	14	15	16	17
February				1	2	3	4	5	6	7	8	9	10	11	12	13	14
March					1	2	3	4	5	6	7	8	9	10	11	12	13
April	1	2	3	4	5	6	7	8	9	10	11	12	13	14	15	16	17
May			1	2	3	4	5	6	7	8	9	10	11	12	13	14	15
June						1	2	3	4	5	6	7	8	9	10	11	12
July	1	2	3	4	5	6	7	8	9	10	11	12	13	14	15	16	17
August				1	2	3	4	5	6	7	8	9	10	11	12	13	14
September							1	2	3	4	5	6	7	8	9	10	11
October		1	2	3	4	5	6	7	8	9	10	11	12	13	14	15	16
November					1	2	3	4	5	6	7	8	9	10	11	12	13
December							1	2	3	4	5	6	7	8	9	10	11

2020

Sat	Sun	Mon	Tue	Wed	Thur	Fri	Sat	Sun	Mon	Tue	Wed	Thur	Fri	Sat	Sun	Mon	Tue	Wed	Thur
18	19	20	21	22	23	24	25	26	27	28	29	30	31						
15	16	17	18	19	20	21	22	23	24	25	26	27	28	29					
14	15	16	17	18	19	20	21	22	23	24	25	26	27	28	29	30	31		
18	19	20	21	22	23	24	25	26	27	28	29	30							
16	17	18	19	20	21	22	23	24	25	26	27	28	29	30	31				
13	14	15	16	17	18	19	20	21	22	23	24	25	26	27	28	29	30		
18	19	20	21	22	23	24	25	26	27	28	29	30	31						
15	16	17	18	19	20	21	22	23	24	25	26	27	28	29	30	31			
12	13	14	15	16	17	18	19	20	21	22	23	24	25	26	27	28	29	30	
17	18	19	20	21	22	23	24	25	26	27	28	29	30	31					
14	15	16	17	18	19	20	21	22	23	24	25	26	27	28	29	30			
12	13	14	15	16	17	18	19	20	21	22	23	24	25	26	27	28	29	30	31

OPERATIONS

All the work you've done so far will give you a sense of the changes that will be required on the operations side of the business. Whether in terms of organization, space, personnel, or technology each change will have an impact on the business and it's important to recognize and, where possible, quantify those impacts.

Each change should be defined as a project with its own goals, scope, cost, and schedule. By listing each project on the following pages, it will be easier to determine which of those projects make the most sense for the business. Include all the potential projects so that no potential improvements are overlooked.

Don't attempt to rate the projects as you make the list. After all the potential projects are listed, we will complete an analysis to establish a rating for each one that will allow you to prioritize them.

Project 1: _____

Benefit: _____

Budget: _____

Start Date: _____

Finish Date: _____

Manager: _____

Rating: Importance___+___=____/Urgency___+___=____

Project 2: _____

Benefit: _____

Budget: _____

Start Date: _____

Finish Date: _____

Manager: _____

Rating: Importance___+___=____/Urgency___+___=____

Project 3: _____

Benefit: _____

Budget: _____

Start Date: _____

Finish Date: _____

Manager: _____

Rating: Importance___+___=____/Urgency___+___=____

Project 4: _____

Benefit: _____

Budget: _____

Start Date: _____

Finish Date: _____

Manager: _____

Rating: Importance___+___=____/Urgency___+___=____

Project 5: _____

Benefit: _____

Budget: _____

Start Date: _____

Finish Date: _____

Manager: _____

Rating: Importance___+___=____/Urgency___+___=____

Project 6: _____

Benefit: _____

Budget: _____

Start Date: _____

Finish Date: _____

Manager: _____

Rating: Importance___+___=____/Urgency___+___=____

Project 7: _____

Benefit: _____

Budget: _____

Start Date: _____

Finish Date: _____

Manager: _____

Rating: Importance___+___=____/Urgency___+___=____

Project 8: _____

Benefit: _____

Budget: _____

Start Date: _____

Finish Date: _____

Manager: _____

Rating: Importance___+___=____/Urgency___+___=____

Project 9: _____

Benefit: _____

Budget: _____

Start Date: _____

Finish Date: _____

Manager: _____

Rating: Importance___+___=____/Urgency___+___=____

Project 10: _____

Benefit: _____

Budget: _____

Start Date: _____

Finish Date: _____

Manager: _____

Rating: Importance___+___=____/Urgency___+___=____

Project 11: _____

Benefit: _____

Budget: _____

Start Date: _____

Finish Date: _____

Manager: _____

Rating: Importance___+___=____/Urgency___+___=____

Project 12: _____

Benefit: _____

Budget: _____

Start Date: _____

Finish Date: _____

Manager: _____

Rating: Importance___+___=____/Urgency___+___=____

Evaluating Options

Decisions are best made based on facts, not emotions. Is it important? Is it urgent? Do you have the time and resources to get it done? Most importantly, will the business benefit over the long run? By assigning values to your options it can become clear which are worth pursuing now and which aren't.

Begin by thinking about how important the project is to the company. Assign a value between 0 and 5 to each Project, with 5 having the highest importance. Now assign a value to the return on investment using the same approach and considering time, resources, systems, etc. For each Project add the two values together. This number will be the level of Importance.

Think next about the urgency of getting each project started – and finished. Will it have an immediate effect on the company's results? Will it keep you from losing customers and market share? Will it help you to retain more customers? Score each Project from 0 to 5 based on that urgency. Now, think about the resources available to devote to the project – time, money, knowledge, software, whatever. Again, for each Project score this on a scale of 0 to 5 with 5 reflecting the fact that you have the resources available immediately. For each Project add the two values together. This number will be the level of Urgency.

On the graph below, plot where each Project lies based on the values you established for Importance and Urgency.

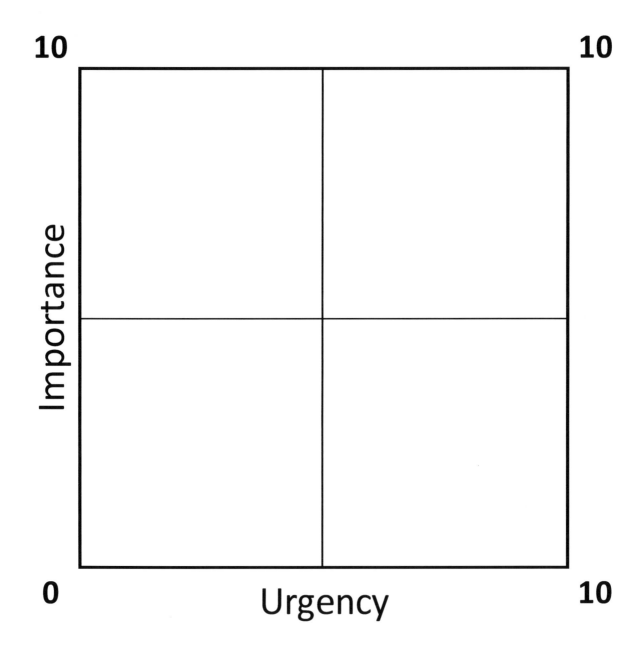

From a strategic standpoint, it makes sense to focus on those projects that lie in the upper right-hand quadrant because they are both important and urgent. If they lie in the upper left-hand quadrant, they might become more urgent or less important as time goes on. They will be worth looking at again in the future. Similarly, in the lower right-hand quadrant, those projects might become more important or less urgent as time goes on.

What the graph clearly shows is that those projects in the lower left-hand quadrant are neither important nor urgent enough to worry about right now. That could change in the future but, for now, they should not be part of the plan.

On your project list mark the projects that you plan to implement. If completing the projects will affect marketing activities, go back to the calendar to block out those project activities.

PEOPLE

Whether you are a business with one employee or a hundred, the fact is that nothing gets accomplished without people. So, one of the most important things to confirm every year is that each person is the right one for the job, and that the job is the right one for that person. This can be particularly difficult with friends and family, but it's a necessary part of the planning. People who don't "fit" are generally not happy or productive in their roles. Being aware of "fit" allows you the time to restructure the work and/or plan for transitions. Remember, these decisions should be based on the business need: "It's not personal, it's Business." Once a decision is made you can address the personal issues with care and consideration.

On the org chart that follows note those areas that need to be addressed and what changes will need to be made. If the change is significant, it might become a project and require more definition. Add those projects to the list you created earlier and rank them as to Importance and Urgency.

The same philosophy should be applied to your professional advisors, vendors/contractors and suppliers. They are also part of your operation and need to be a good fit.

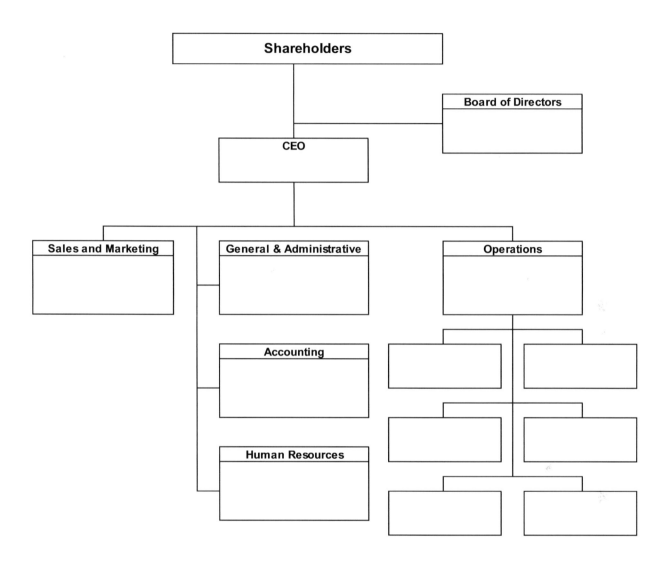

TAKING ACTION

Believe it or not, you've created a strategy for moving forward toward your long-term goals. Now that you've done the hard part – the thinking – all that remains is to put your plan into action. You will need to fill in the details, finalize the schedule and review progress on a regular basis.

Take the time now to transfer your ideas to the following pages. In the calendar, schedule a review every three months. This is a plan based on what you know now. What you know three months from now will be different and the plan might need to be updated. The same holds true for six and nine months from now. The good news is that it will not require starting from scratch because you've done the proper planning.

2020 Strategic Plan for

_____

Our Mission is

_____

_____

_____

Our Vision is

_____

_____

_____

Our Values are

_____

_____

_____

Our Revenue Goal is _____

With a Net Income of _____

We will achieve our Revenue Goal by focusing on the following revenue streams:

_____

_____

_____

_____

Our target market is:

_____

_____

_____

We will reach are target market with the following marketing strategies:

_____

_____

_____

_____

Our Operations will be improved through implementation of the following Projects:

_____

_____

_____

_____

To be more efficient and effective we are planning the following changes within the organization:

_____

_____

_____

_____

_____

_____

Based on our current plan, we are targeting future years Revenue and Net Income as follows:

2021 Revenue_____ Net Income_____

2022 Revenue_____ Net Income_____

2023 Revenue_____ Net Income_____

2024 Revenue_____ Net Income_____

The following dates and actions are critical to our success:

_____

_____

_____

_____

_____

_____

WHAT IF'S

The best laid plans can go awry when things happen that we can't control. There will often be an emotional response, but action should be taken based on facts and analysis - what would the best course of action be based on the available facts? People tend to be optimistic – more like in denial - about negative possibilities. You ignore such possibilities to your detriment.

If you buy oceanfront property in the southeastern United States, you might not factor in the possibility of hurricane damage. After all, this location hasn't had a hurricane strike in 15 years. That doesn't decrease the possibility of a strike, it increases the probability of experiencing a loss. The fact is that a strike has occurred every (fill in the blank) years on average over the past century. If you add in the effects of climate change, the probability of damage increases. If you purchased that property, you might want to consider taking action to mitigate potential losses.

What concerns might you have? Some that come to mind are:
- Natural disasters or weather damage
- Losses due to fire or water
- Data breach or loss
- Product or process liability
- Losing key personnel
- Criminal activity
- Regulatory changes or changes to law

Just as we can calculate a probable return on investment for marketing activities, we can follow a similar approach to analyze the what if's in business. The advantage of the approach is that it's a thought experiment and you don't have to spend any money until it makes sense to do so. You could have a key employee that is considering another opportunity, or an employee that gets pregnant and will take maternity leave, or you need more space or less, or you need to add a product or service, or you might lose a major customer, etc.

The process is straightforward. Take any scenario you are concerned about and describe it. What are the potential positive aspects, Pros? What are the concerns, Cons? If there are costs associated with the approach, what are they? If there are financial benefits, what are they? What's the probability of the event or outcome you envision ever happening? Then, based on the dollars and probability, what's the financial risk or reward? Finally, based on all this information, what approach could you take? In general, your approach will be to either ignore, monitor, mitigate, or resolve any potential concern.

Think of this as a pencil exercise. As you develop the information, your thinking on the matter will evolve and you will need an eraser to make the changes. As you refine your approach, you might think of additional tasks and costs. Timing will change. The changes might result in efficiencies that generate revenue. Remember, the whole point of the exercise is to think through the issues in detail before you commit to a plan - and to avoid having your emotions drive your decisions. The sunrise might be beautiful over the ocean, but hurricanes also arise in the east.

Use the following worksheets to sketch out the scenarios when they concern you. Pay attention to the calculated financial risk. Low dollar amounts aren't worth worrying about because the impact is small. Don't let them keep you up at night. High dollar financial risk items might require a mitigation strategy - so you will be able to sleep.

What if _____

_____

The Positive Aspects are _____

_____

_____

_____

The Concerns are _____

_____

_____

_____

The Calculated Risk is

_____ - _____ = _____ X _____ = _____
Income or Savings   Expenses   Net Impact   Probability   Calculated Risk

Our approach will be _____

_____

_____

_____

Action: ☐ Ignore   ☐ Monitor   ☐ Mitigate   ☐ Resolve

What if _____

_____

The Positive Aspects are _____

_____

_____

_____

The Concerns are _____

_____

_____

_____

The Calculated Risk is

_____ - _____ = _____ X _____ = _____
Income or Savings   Expenses   Net Impact   Probability   Calculated Risk

Our approach will be _____

_____

_____

_____

Action: ☐ Ignore   ☐ Monitor   ☐ Mitigate   ☐ Resolve

What if _____

_____

The Positive Aspects are _____

_____

_____

_____

The Concerns are _____

_____

_____

_____

The Calculated Risk is

_____ - _____ = _____ X _____ = _____
Income or Savings   Expenses   Net Impact   Probability   Calculated Risk

Our approach will be _____

_____

_____

_____

Action: ☐ Ignore ☐ Monitor ☐ Mitigate ☐ Resolve

What if _____

_____

The Positive Aspects are _____

_____

_____

_____

The Concerns are _____

_____

_____

_____

The Calculated Risk is

_____ - _____ = _____ X _____ = _____
Income or Savings   Expenses   Net Impact   Probability   Calculated Risk

Our approach will be _____

_____

_____

_____

Action: ☐ Ignore   ☐ Monitor   ☐ Mitigate   ☐ Resolve

What if _____

_____

The Positive Aspects are _____

_____

_____

_____

The Concerns are _____

_____

_____

_____

The Calculated Risk is

_____ - _____ = _____ X _____ = _____

Income or Savings   Expenses   Net Impact   Probability   Calculated Risk

Our approach will be _____

_____

_____

_____

Action: ☐ Ignore   ☐ Monitor   ☐ Mitigate   ☐ Resolve

What if _____

_____

The Positive Aspects are _____

_____

_____

_____

The Concerns are _____

_____

_____

_____

The Calculated Risk is

_____ - _____ = _____ X _____ = _____
Income or Savings   Expenses   Net Impact   Probability   Calculated Risk

Our approach will be _____

_____

_____

_____

Action: ☐ Ignore   ☐ Monitor   ☐ Mitigate   ☐ Resolve

What if _____

_____

The Positive Aspects are _____

_____

_____

_____

The Concerns are _____

_____

_____

_____

The Calculated Risk is

_____ - _____ = _____ X _____ = _____

Income or Savings   Expenses   Net Impact   Probability   Calculated Risk

Our approach will be _____

_____

_____

_____

Action: ☐ Ignore   ☐ Monitor   ☐ Mitigate   ☐ Resolve

What if _____

_____

The Positive Aspects are _____

_____

_____

_____

The Concerns are _____

_____

_____

_____

The Calculated Risk is

_____ - _____ = _____ X _____ = _____

Income or Savings   Expenses   Net Impact   Probability   Calculated Risk

Our approach will be _____

_____

_____

_____

Action: ☐ Ignore   ☐ Monitor   ☐ Mitigate   ☐ Resolve

What if _____

_____

The Positive Aspects are _____

_____

_____

_____

The Concerns are _____

_____

_____

_____

The Calculated Risk is

_____ - _____ = _____ X _____ = _____
Income or Savings   Expenses   Net Impact   Probability   Calculated Risk

Our approach will be _____

_____

_____

_____

Action: ☐ Ignore ☐ Monitor ☐ Mitigate ☐ Resolve

What if _____

_____

The Positive Aspects are _____

_____

_____

_____

The Concerns are _____

_____

_____

_____

The Calculated Risk is

_____ - _____ = _____ X _____ = _____
Income or Savings   Expenses   Net Impact   Probability   Calculated Risk

Our approach will be _____

_____

_____

_____

Action: ☐ Ignore   ☐ Monitor   ☐ Mitigate   ☐ Resolve

ABOUT THE AUTHOR

Dave Ferguson has spent over 30 years coaching hundreds of people in business: helping them to work smarter, not harder; to be more effective, focused, and strategic in their approach. He has owned small businesses in the past, but it was his years of experience in corporate operations, working for companies large and small - and especially the fact that the last company invited him to "go out and find something else to do" - that led him to open Lake County Business Coaching, Inc. in 2005. In addition to working with his business clients he has contributed his time as a counselor at the Small Business Development Center at the College of Lake County and as an Assistant Director for BNI.

Dave lives in Libertyville, Illinois with his wife. He has three adult children and a granddaughter. He is an active networker, a member of the GLMV Chamber of Commerce and the Small Business Advocacy Council, a speaker, teacher, and author. Both LakeCountyBusinessCoaching.com and his free monthly newsletter provide valuable tools and tips to help people in business improve their performance. You can follow him on Facebook and Twitter and connect on LinkedIn.

Visit LakeCountyBusinessCoaching.com for business information, tips, contact information and to request electronic copies of the spreadsheets used for the forms in the workbook.

NOTES

NOTES

NOTES

NOTES

NOTES

NOTES

NOTES

NOTES

NOTES

NOTES

NOTES

71824517R00058